AF270586

CATS

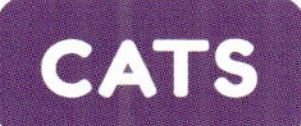

CALICO CATS

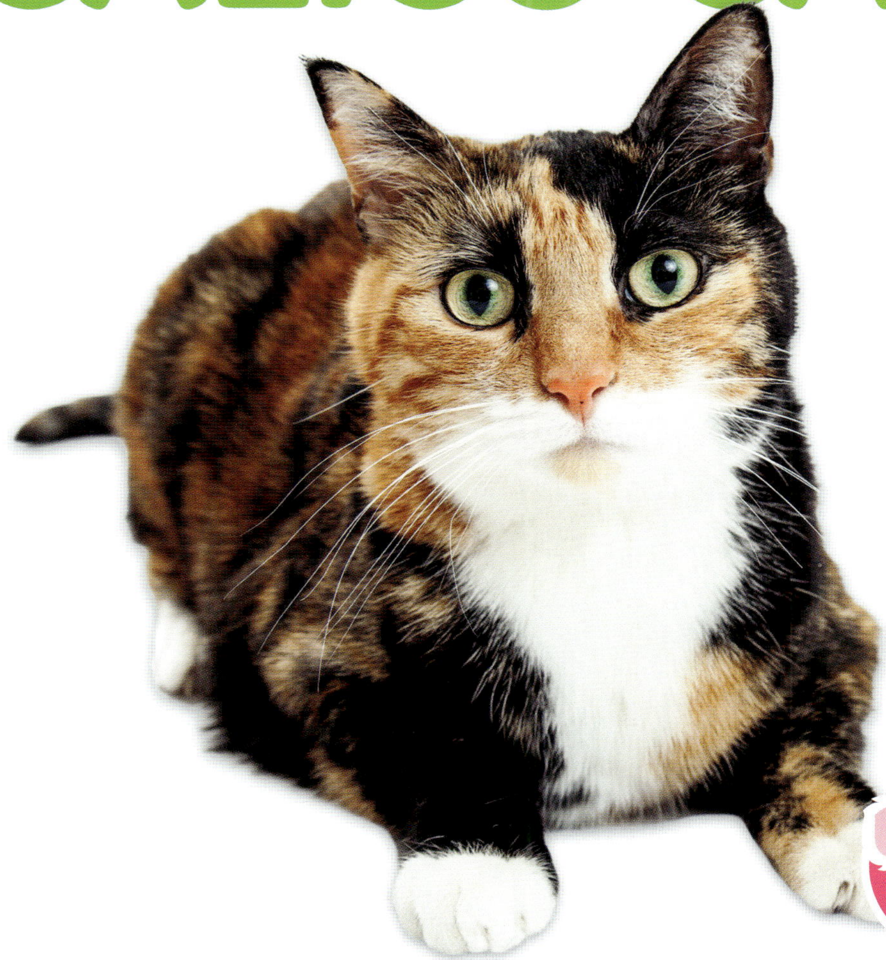

by Elizabeth Andrews

Cody Koala
An Imprint of Pop!
popbooksonline.com

Hello! My name is Cody Koala

This book is filled with videos, puzzles, games, and more! Scan the QR codes* while you read, or visit the website below to make this book pop.

popbooksonline.com/calico

*Scanning QR codes requires a web-enabled smart device with a QR code reader app and a camera.

abdobooks.com

Published by Pop!, a division of ABDO, PO Box 398166, Minneapolis, Minnesota 55439. Copyright ©2023 by Abdo Consulting Group, Inc. International copyrights reserved in all countries. No part of this book may be reproduced in any form without written permission from the publisher. Cody Koala™ is a trademark and logo of Pop!.

Printed in the United States of America, North Mankato, Minnesota.
102022
012023

THIS BOOK CONTAINS RECYCLED MATERIALS

Cover Photo: Shutterstock Images
Interior Photos: Shutterstock and Getty Images
Editor: Grace Hansen
Series Designer: Colleen McLaren

Library of Congress Control Number: 2022941104

Publisher's Cataloging-in-Publication Data
Names: Andrews, Elizabeth, author.
Title: Calico cats / by Elizabeth Andrews
Description: Minneapolis, Minnesota : Pop!, 2023 | Series: Cats | Includes online resources and index.
Identifiers: ISBN 9781098243104 (lib. bdg.) | ISBN 9781098243807 (ebook)
Subjects: LCSH: Calico cats--Juvenile literature. | Cat, Domestic--Juvenile literature. | Shorthair cat--Juvenile literature. | Zoology--Juvenile literature.
Classification: DDC 636.83--dc23

Table of Contents

Chapter 1

Seeing Spots!

The calico cat is not a **breed**. It is simply a lovely coat pattern. Nearly all cat breeds have the chance to be a calico!

Watch a video here!

Exotic shorthair
British shorthair
Maine coon

No matter the breed, a calico's soft fur should have at least three colors. The most basic is white, black, and orange.

Male calico cats are very
rare. Only about one in 3,000
calico cats are male. Female
cats are more likely to be born
with **genes** that make the
coat pattern.

Chapter 2

Personality

Calico cats do not have any set personality traits. A Persian calico cat might be very lazy. A Manx calico cat might be more playful.

Learn more here!

Cats will also have personalities that match their **environment**. If there are young, playful kids in a calico cat's home, it might have more energy too.

Many calico cat owners say that their cats have strong and spunky personalities.

Chapter 3

Cat Care

Cats are naturally clean animals. They use their scratchy tongues to wash themselves. Calico cats should still be brushed weekly. Their **litter boxes** must be cleaned daily.

15

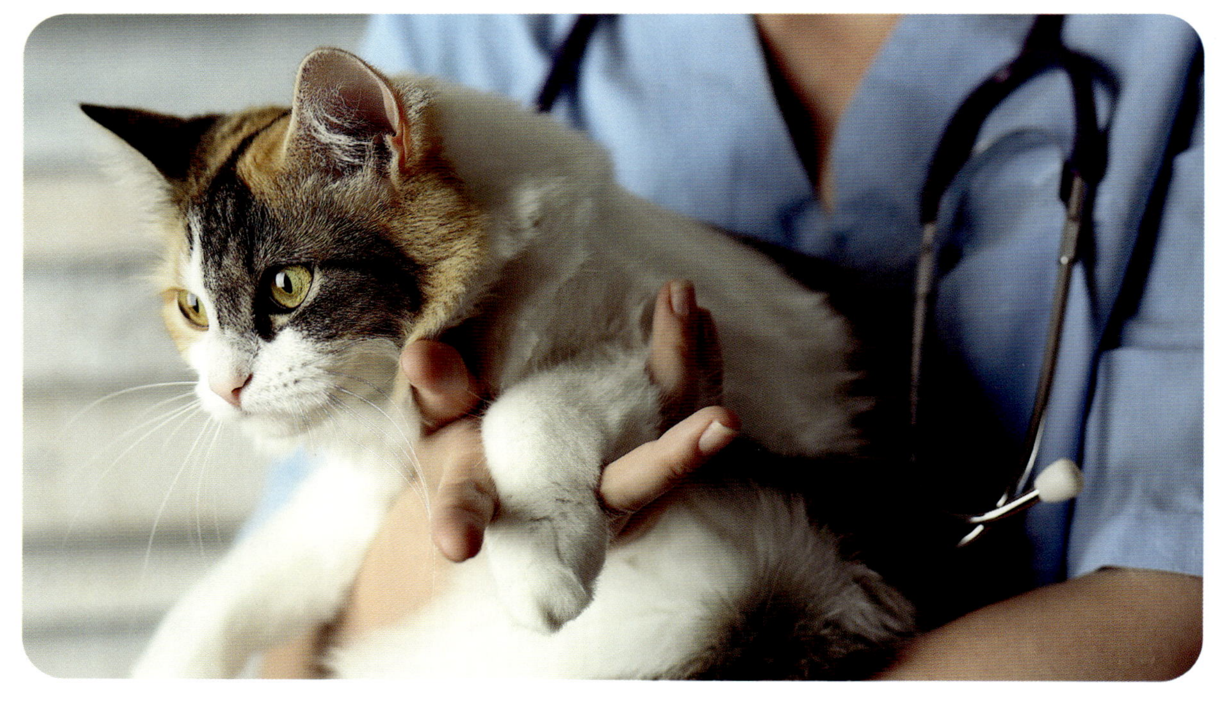

Female calico cats are usually healthy. They still need to visit the vet once a year for a checkup.

Male calico cats are more likely to be unhealthy. They may need more special care from a vet.

Calico kittens are special. There are not full **litters** of calico kittens. But litters may include a calico. Kittens stay with their mother for 12 to 16 weeks.

Chapter 4

Lucky Kitty

Because calico cats cannot be planned, people consider them lucky. Any person with a beautiful calico cat for a pet should feel lucky!

Complete an
activity here!

Calico cats are the official cat
of Maryland! Their colors match
Maryland's state flag colors.

Making Connections

Text-to-Self

What breed of calico cat would you want to own?

Text-to-Text

Have you read any other books that talk about cat coat patterns? How were they similar to or different from the calico pattern?

Text-to-World

Calico cats are thought to be lucky! Are there any other lucky animals in the world?

Glossary

breed – a particular type or kind of animal; to develop animals to act and look a specific way.

gene – information in DNA that affects how animals look and behave.

environment – the things and conditions that are all around one.

litter – all kittens born at one time to a mother cat.

litter box – a box filled with cat litter, which is like sand. Cats use litter boxes to bury their waste.

rare – not often found or seen.

Index

Online Resources

popbooksonline.com

Thanks for reading this Cody Koala book!

This book is filled with videos, puzzles, games, and more! Scan the QR codes* while you read, or visit the website below to make this book pop.

popbooksonline.com/calico

*Scanning QR codes requires a web-enabled smart device with a QR code reader app and a camera.